Book of Country

Furniture, Baskets, Stoneware and More

Don and Carol Raycraft

COLLECTOR BOOKS

A Division of Schroeder Publishing Co., Inc.

The current values in this book should be used only as a guide. They are not intended to set prices, which vary from one section of the country to another. Auction prices as well as dealer prices vary greatly and are affected by condition as well as demand. Neither the Author nor the Publisher assumes responsibility for any losses that might be incurred as a result of consulting this guide.

ACKNOWLEDGEMENTS

Lee and Cindy Sawyer
Dwight and Arvilla Doss
Elmer and Merrilyn Fedder
Bob and Judy Farling
Jack Thomas
S. I. Salowitz
Dr. Alex Hood
Opal and Joe Pickens
John and Virginia Curry
Bill Schroeder
Steve Quertermous
Dr. David Fylipek
Marjorie Bush
Betty Spilman
Dr. Cutter
Edna Faulkner

PHOTOGRAPHY

Jon Balke
Carol Raycraft
Elmer Fedder
Howard Bush
Bob Farling
R. Craig Raycraft
Peter DelSignore
Andrew Tucker
T. T. Argyle

INTRODUCTION

When we first began collecting country antiques in the mid-1960's, the biggest difficulty we encountered was identifying the pieces we found. At that point, there was not a national mania for American antiques that surfaced in a multitude of magazines and books. There were articles on Pilgrim century furniture and books filled with pictures taken of museum quality room settings. This did not assist us in our quest because the shops we visited did not carry seventeenth and eighteenth century furniture.

By chance we found a copy of Mary Earle Gould's classic book, *Early American Woodenware*, that was originally published in 1942. Eventually we began a correspondence with Miss Gould that continued until her death. She sent us copies of her books on the early American house and tinware. In each of these volumes she stressed that houses and antiques should be left in their natural state as much as possible. In the 1960's, most pieces of pine furniture that we found had long since been separated from their painted finish. Pieces that had not been stripped were in little demand outside a small group of collectors who were a decade ahead of everyone else.

The first time we visited a home that was filled with painted furniture and accessories, we left with mixed emotions. Country antiques that retain their original or early finish often require a period of adjustment before the love affair can begin. A cupboard that has only a portion of its paint is not necessarily desirable. The finish on the piece should be reasonably intact. If a portion of the door has been stripped or the paint on a side has been lost from exposure in a damp basement, the piece may have to be refinished. With the sudden increase of interest in painted furniture, there has been a tendency to put pieces in homes and national magazines that have been seriously flawed. A decade ago the piece would have been instantly and correctly refinished; but, today, if the paint remains, the owner often adds it to the permanent collection regardless of condition. There is a fine line between an early finish that can be restored and one that is so battered it is not worth retaining.

The growing love affair with painted finishes has made it a necessity for colletors to become aware of a new vocabulary. A finish can be described as original, early, "moved around", or enhanced.

The original paint is the initial coat that was put on shortly after it was made. Rarely do collectors find a piece that carries only a single, original coat of paint. Most country furniture was made of pine or poplar. Pine and poplar furniture was seldom left without paint because it kept the wood from splintering, added some color to the room, helped preserve the wood, and made it simpler to clean.

"Early" paint followed the original paint and may be two or three coats thick. "Early" is an imprecise description because it is relative to the age of the piece.

Paint that has been "moved around" or enhanced on a cupboard or dry sink should be carefully studied before the check is written. If a cupboard has a worn surface, it is possible to use a commercial stripper to turn the century old paint that remains into a semi-paste. The old paint is then "moved around" with a brush to cover the entire piece. If the owner is asked if the paint is "early", he can semi-truthfully reply in the affirmative.

"Enhanced" is a kind term used to describe a technique that many of us do to our homes every fourth spring. A cupboard that has been "enhanced" has its existing paint touched up to the point that it appears to be in pristine condition. Gifted enhancers can take the trouble to wipe paint off areas (tabletops, drawer pulls) that would receive significant wear. This gives additional "age" to the piece. We see furniture, sugar buckets, bowls, and churns that have been "enhanced" at every antique show we attend. Some of the jobs are done at a highly skilled level and others appear to be executed with a broom dipped in latex.

The great case pieces that had their paint removed a generation ago are reappearing today with the "original" paint magically restored. Several gifted paint enhancers do nothing else but work on high ticket items for select dealers. Keep in mind that an exceptional pine step-back cupboard with a blind front (no glass) could be worth $1,000.00 to $1,200.00 if it has been tastefully refinished. The same cupboard in a spectacular blue paint could be priced in the $3,000.00 to $4,000.00 range. The temptation to turn the refinished cupboard into a painted cupboard is too great and too easy for some dealers to resist and there are a wealth of customers searching for blue cupboards.

Books and Shows

Twenty years ago, we passed up some exceptional things because we didn't know what they were. A stoneware grease lamp for $22.00 and a set of six balloon-back chairs for $500.00 come quickly to mind among a long and lamented list. At that point there were no magazines or newspapers devoted to primitives (country had not entered the collecting language) and few books were being written. The price guides were devoted to carnival glass and napkin rings and we read *Antiques Journal* and *Spinning Wheel*. On occasion a rare article that interested us appeared.

We anxiously anticipated antiques shows that were held in Pennsylvania, Ohio and Indiana. The Crutcher shows in Indianappolis especially appealed to us and we replayed Christmas Eve and the long wait to Christmas morning before each trip. There weren't shows fifty-two weekends a year and each was a special event with dealers who traveled long distances to display their wares. The situation today has changed a bit with monthly antiques shows held in every town in America that has running water.

The dealers who do the shows have large investments of time and capital. They have costs that include travel, lodging, meals and booth rent. They also have to devote more time and money to finding antiques to offer for sale. The number of individual shops has probably diminished with a corresponding rise in the frequency of shows. Few dealers can afford to rent commercial space, advertise, pay utility bills and earn a profit. The dealers must turn to shows and flea markets as an alternative to maintaining an antiques shop with regular hours. Show promotors have a large number of dealers who want to sell antiques and are willing to pay for the opportunity. The promoter secures a building, advertises, and sells tickets at the door. On rare occasions everyone involved makes money.

In recent years, several books and periodicals have had a profound influence on the buying habits of thousands of collectors. They have created a new market for contemporary folk art that did not exist before.

CONTEMPORARY FOLK ART

The debate over what constitutes "folk art" and what does not will not be settled by this slim volume. Historically, folk or "naive" art was created by an untrained but skillful artisan who produced quilts, coverlets, samplers, baskets, carvings, woodenware, trade signs and a wide variety of other items for himself/herself or to sell or barter for small sums. The debate still rages in some quarters whether or not factory-made windmill weights or weathervanes can be classified as folk art. We think not.

There is no question that "early American" towel holders decorated with hearts and pineapples applied with a wood burner do not fall within the folk art category.

The last several years have seen an explosion of folk art shows across the nation. They are conducted much like a conventional antiques show with booths, dealers, previews, and extensive advertising. These shows have been successful because they provide a reasonably priced alternative to country antiques. The investment potential is generally limited because of the huge quantities of most of the items that are produced. The best contemporary folk pieces are not inexpensive and are made by gifted artists who strictly control their offerings.

The shows have also been sanctioned by the growing number of periodicals that display rooms decorated with antiques and contemporary folk art. The key to buying contemporary folk art is to maintain the same level of selectivity you would apply when purchasing country antiques.

ORGANIZATION

This book is a shade unconventional in the manner in which it is put together because we have not designed it around specific chapters that include baskets, stoneware, furniture, textiles, toys, woodenware and advertising. We are going to take a leisurely route through the field of American country antiques and point out some exceptional pieces along the way.

A book like this, to be effective, must provide illustrations of country furniture and accessories that are still available to collectors. All of the items pictured on the pages that follow have been taken in the houses of friends or from our own collection. We have always hesitated to use pictures of museum collections because it produces a less than realistic view of what is available today.

The contemporary folk art that is included has been chosen with special care. A decade ago, the market for contemporary folk art was just beginning. Country antiques were still being offered within a price range that most collectors could manage and there were few shows that emphasized newer items.

Putting the early and the late into tasteful and satisfying combinations is a difficult and complex task. Hopefully, this book will provide some information, insight and enjoyment. It is impossible to read a single book or visit a home or restoration and walk away with all the answers. Understanding the field of American country antiques is a life long pursuit that generally generates more questions that answers.

Unusual pine cupboard with drawers and storage bins, c. 1870's.

Pine step-back cupboard, painted red, mid-nineteenth century, paneled doors. A step-back cupboard has a recessed upper section that provides a work area or shelf. This particular cupboard was made in two pieces so it could be easily transported. The paneled doors in the upper section also make it a blind front. If the doors had glass or lights it could be called a glazed front cupboard. Generally a cupboard with lights is more expensive than a comparable blind front.

Refinished Norwegian cupboard, pine, c. mid-nineteenth century.

The three painted pine cupboards all date from the first half of the nineteenth century. The two open or pewter cupboards contain no doors. An open cupboard is a highly desirable piece of country furniture that is rarely found in its original form. Many of the open cupboards we see originally had doors. It is simpler to transform either a blind or glazed front cupboard into an open cupboard than make a new door for one that has been misplaced or damaged beyond repair. Matching the paint or finish of the cupboard with the new door can also be difficult. A careful study of the front of the open cupboard could reveal screw holes or excessive wear where the original hinges that held the missing doors were located.

Chimney cupboards are often made of pine and were used for storage. This refinished cupboard dates from the 1860-1875 period.

Refinished step-back cupboard, probably Midwestern, c. 1870's.

Painted pine open cupboard, c. mid-nineteenth century.

Late nineteenth century child's dish dresser or cupboard.

Poplar jelly cupboard, found in the Valley of Virginia, c. mid-nineteenth century.

Pine open cupboard from Virginia, c. 1860.

Step-back cupboard in green paint, c. 1840's.

North Carolina open cupboard, unusual size, c. 1840. The oval rug is a contemporary piece done by Mrs. F.L. Beck.

Refinished pine open cupboard, possibly English in origin.

New England chimney cupboard with early red paint, c. 1860.

Pine farm table with scrubbed top and blue base from North Carolina, c. 1850.

The blue-grey hanging cupboard dates from 1840-1860 and was found in New York State.

This pie safe is unusual because it has two upper drawers and a single large drawer below. Pie or kitchen safes were designed for food storage and tend to be found more in the Midwest than any other section of the nation. Pine and poplar were commonly used and oak and walnut safes can occasionally be found. Many were factory-made after 1870.

Pine pie safe with hand-punched heart tins, from Virginia, c. 1850. The contemporary folk art horse pull-toy was made by Martha Woodard of Chesapeake, Virginia.

Pennsylvania hired man's bed, c. 1840-1860, pine with maple rails, original red paint. We bought this bed out of a chicken house near Adamstown, Pennsylvania.

Low post bed, maple and pine, red "wash", c. 1860-1870's.

High post country bed, pine and maple, found in Virginia, c. 1830-1840. The six-board blanket box has blue-green paint and turned feet. It is a product of the mid-nineteenth century and is made of pine.

Early nineteenth century sugar chest in old blue paint, found in Virginia.

Pennsylvania blanket box, six-board construction, bun feet, original blue paint, c. 1850-1860.

Six-board blanket box, painted a strong blue, dove-tailed sides, c. 1870.

Six-board blanket box in bittersweet paint, New York State, c. 1850-1860's. We bought this blanket box at a rummage sale in the basement of a church in Bloomington, Illinois, in 1984. Early one July evening, a friend called and described a six-board box in paint that he had seen in an unlikely place. When we reluctantly agreed to turn off the television set and drive over to see the box, we did it as a favor for a friend. We knew there was no way it could be what he described. The church basement was filled with "antiques" collectors who were loading up on salt and pepper shakers, linens, half-filled tubes of tooth paste, and pastel leisure suits. In the middle of the room was a six-board box in bittersweet paint that elicited little interest. As fast as we could manage it, we added it to the permanent collection.

Mid-nineteenth century blanket box of pine that has been repainted by Wisconsin artist Lou Shifferel.

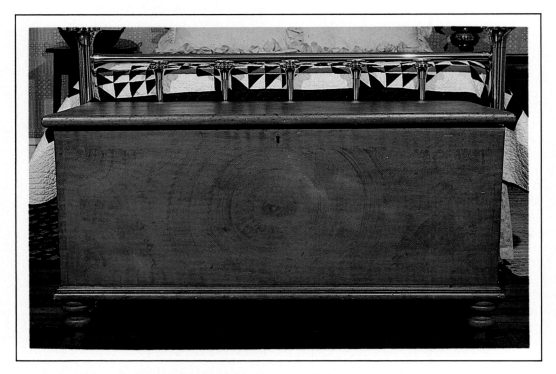

Grain painted six-board blanket box, c. 1850-1860, probably from Pennsylvania.

Pine dry sink with uncommonly extended trough, Pennsylvania, c. mid-nineteenth century.

Simple pine dry sink, found in New York State, c. 1860.

Painted pine dry sink with storage drawers, c. 1870.

Pine bucket bench with shelves mortised into sides, found in Illinois, painted, c. 1880.

Pine bucket bench, nailed construction, Virginia, c. 1900.

Walnut desk, c. 1860-1880, probably Midwestern in origin.

Pine and cherry plantation desk from Virginia, c. mid-nineteenth century. It is difficult to determine provenance with country furniture because few pieces were kept for later generations. As factory-made furniture became increasingly available, the earlier hand-crafted examples of pine were stored or given away. This desk was purchased from the family of a physician who used it during the 1845-1865 period. The contemporary folk painting was done by Virginia Beach, Virginia, artist, Mary Myers.

Pine lift-top desk, early blue-green paint, c. 1820-1840.

Pennsylvania school master's desk with lift-top, painted red with stenciled legs, dovetailed box, c. mid-nineteenth century.

Late nineteenth century rocking chair in red paint, Zoar, Ohio.

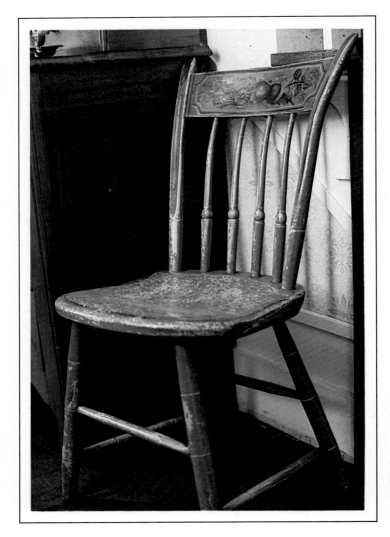

Painted spindle-back chair, stenciled crest rail, splayed legs, pine plank seat, c. 1860's.

Refinished rocking chair, hand-crafted, c. 1860's.

Country sofa, maple, factory-made, c. 1880's.

Half-spindle back kitchen chair, sold in sets of six or eight, factory-made, c. 1880, stenciled crest rail.

Mammy's bench with original gate that kept the baby from rolling off, maple with pine seat, decorated crest rail, c. 1860.

Shaker No. 7 rocking chair, Mt. Lebanon, New York, maple, c. late nineteenth century.

Country child's arm chair of maple; mid-nineteenth century side chair in blue paint with a rush seat.

Ladder-back chair and pine step-back cupboard from the Valley of Virginia, both mid-nineteenth century.

Pine saw-buck work table, found in Ohio, c. late nineteenth century, scrubbed top.

Refinished side or lamp table, c. 1870, probably Midwestern.

Walnut and pine farm table, 7 ft. long, found in Virginia, c. 1870.

Carpenter's table, c. twentieth century, maple.

Salt glazed stoneware butter churn with slip-trailed bird decoration, c. 1870's.

Slip-cupping or trailing was a technique used for decorating stoneware in the mid-nineteenth century. Slip is a mixture of clay, water and ground cobalt for color that was used with a brush or slip-cup to decorate stoneware. The slip-trailing process left a raised pattern on the surface of the stoneware.

This stoneware jar was a product of the C.W. Braun pottery of Buffalo, New York. It dates from the 1860's. The potter's mark was impressed into the surface before the clay hardened.

The bird on the Braun jar was drawn with a slip-cup. It is interesting to speculate precisely what bird the decorator had in mind on this jar. Many times the tail feathers, beak, body and feet of two or three varieties will be combined. Decorators were often paid on a piece rate rather than by the hour or day. They were highly motivated to generate quantity and, unless a piece was specially ordered, quality was an after thought. This was especially true after the 1870's when competition reached the point that cobalt decoration on stoneware was kept to a minimum.

J. & E. Norton, Bennington, Vermont, crock with slip-trailed house, fence and pine tree, 1850-1859. Scenes are rarely found on stoneware crocks or jugs. Some of the most elaborately decorated pieces of American stoneware were made at Bennington during the 1850-1859 period of ownership by Julius and Edward Norton. Collectors of stoneware usually have an advantage over other collectors of country antiques because a potter's mark impressed into the pieces can give a quasi-accurate date of its production. The potter's name and location make it fairly simple to isolate the time frame in which he was in operation. Marks that were in use only for a single year are not uncommon because potters were notorious for losing their business due to a kiln explosion or periodic bankruptcy.

The house, fence and the bird on a branch were created with a slip-cup and are a rare and interesting combination on this crock. It is quite possible that this piece was decorated to show the range of scenes that was available for purchase.

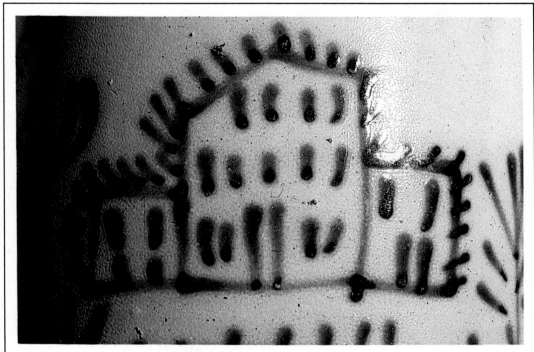

Stoneware decorators could not take the time to do an architect's rendering of a mid-nineteenth century home. The slashes of cobalt that serve as doors and windows are about as close as he could get.

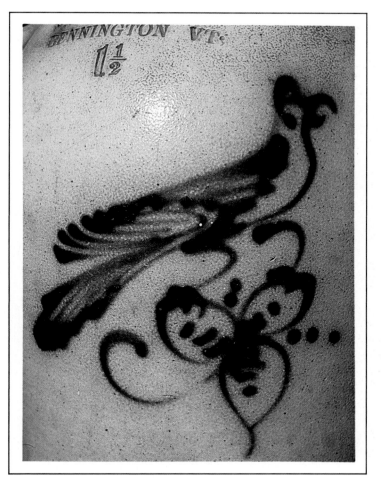

The J. Norton & Co. mark on this stoneware jar is a fairly rare mark because it was only in use for three years, from 1859 to 1861. The impressed "1½" is a capacity mark. Norton made similar jars in seven sizes during his period of ownership.

The chicken pecking corn was done with a slip cup on this crock in the 1870's. The chickens who peck corn on nineteenth century stoneware invariably do the pecking to their right. Rarely will a piece be found that displays a "left-pecking chicken". The decorators who anonymously painted stoneware in the mid-nineteenth century moved on occasion from pottery to pottery and took their designs with them. It is not uncommon to find identical birds on stoneware from several different potteries.

This finely done robin was outlined with a slip-cup and then finished with a brush on a four gallon crock from Ft. Edward, New York. The three primary factors in evaluating a piece of stoneware are decoration, condition and maker's mark. This particular piece has excellent decoration, a fairly common mark and is not cracked or chipped. Serious stoneware collectors become more tolerant of condition as the quality of the decoration increases. For example, this is a good piece of stoneware but not a great one. To maintain its value, it will have to be in almost perfect condition. If the decoration was a sinking battleship with a man carrying a flag on the deck, it could be severely cracked and still be eagerly sought by collectors.

Slip-trailed blue birds that could be drawn quickly were a standard feature of most stoneware potteries. The decoration did not make the stoneware a more useful product. Its purpose was only to catch the potential customer's eye and lead to a sale. The decorators were not trained artists but simple "folk" who needed a job and had some skill with a slip-cup or brush.

This slip-trailed duck is flapping its wings on a four gallon crock from the W. Hart Pottery of Ogdensburgh, New York. It dates from the late 1870's.

In the 1960's we were often faced with the dilemma of selecting from a wide variety of $50.00 "bird" crocks similar to these examples. Unfortunately, we were too selective and didn't borrow some money, back up a truck, rent a warehouse, write some $50.00 checks, wait twenty years, and hold an auction.

Jerry Beaumont of York, Maine, is a gifted potter who produces the finest reproduction stoneware of the twentieth century. The jar at right is Beaumont's adaptation of the 1850-1859 J. & E. Norton decoration of the deer, spruce tree and fence.

The stoneware Teddy bears and the cat are also made by Jerry Beaumont in limited quantities. These pieces were molded rather than individually hand-thrown on a potter's wheel. In the late nineteenth century, country potteries began to close because they could not face the competition of national companies that distributed their products all over the country. These potteries molded their crocks and jugs and quickly decorated them with a stencil rather than hand throwing, brushing or slip-cupping.

Miniature stoneware churns, crocks, jugs, and jars that have been individually thrown and decorated with brushed cobalt.

The stoneware jug at left can be dated by its shape. It can best be described as ovoid or pear-shaped in form. The first stoneware thrown in the United States was made in this fashion. This piece dates from the 1830's or early 1840's. As the nineteenth century wore on, stoneware gradually became more cylindrical in form. The Connecticut stoneware jar at right is from the same period. An interesting comparison can be made between the ovoid jug and the J. & E. Norton "bird on a stump" jug next to it. The Norton piece has cylindrical sides and dates about thirty years after the ovoid example.

Much of the stoneware from western Pennsylvania that was made after 1875 was heavily stenciled rather than decorated by hand. This eight gallon storage jar was made at the Williams and Reppert Pottery of Greensboro, Pennsylvania. The stenciled eagle is complemented by a hand-brushed capacity mark and swirls. The combination of stencil and brushing on the same piece is not common.

This representative sampling of American decorated stoneware includes cake crocks, a spittoon, jugs, crocks, jars and a pitcher. All of the pieces are hand-thrown and date from the nineteenth century with two exceptions. Take a close look and pick out the two contemporary pieces of stoneware.

Stoneware butter churn, applied "ear" handles, c. 1880's, no maker's mark.

The first pottery made in colonial America was earthenware or red-ware. The red clay was fired at a lower temperature than stoneware and was available in huge quantities that could be dug with a shovel. The slip decorated pie plate at right is from Pennsylvania and dates from the mid-nineteenth century.

Redware milk pan and pitcher, both unglazed on the exterior, Pennsylvania, c. mid-nineteenth century.

There are a multitude of examples of molded stoneware that was mass produced after 1850. As America gradually became industrialized and the migration into new areas continued, there was a need for household goods that could be purchased rather than hand-made. Local potters suffered and gave up their businesses as mail order houses appeared with catalogs in the 1870's. A sponge dipped in cobalt was used to decorate these pieces of molded stoneware that date from about 1900.

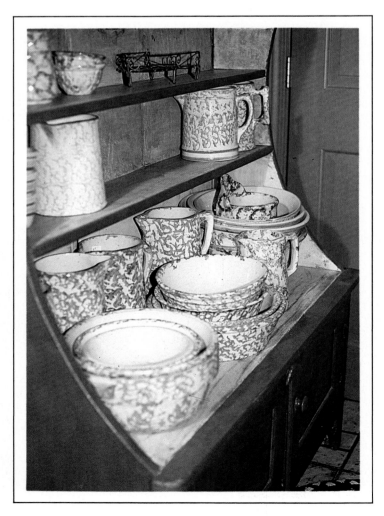

Sponge-decorated stoneware or spongeware, c. 1900.

Molded stoneware was also decorated with a mottled brown and yellow glaze called Rockingham. The Bennington potteries were famous for their wares in the late 1840's and other makers in Ohio quickly followed with very similar examples. The vast majority of the Rockingham plates, pitchers and bowls were unsigned.

Collection of mid-nineteenth century Rockingham pottery.

Stoneware pigs, c. 1900.

More examples of Rockingham pottery.

Between 1860 and the early 1900's, a large number of American and English potteries manufactured ironstone tableware for households and hotels. The huge quantities that were purchased in the late nineteenth century are still being collected today.

Graniteware pitcher and bowl set, early twentieth century.

Premium jug given away by a grocery store in Altoona, Pennsylvania, c. late nineteenth century. The writing was incised into the front of the stoneware jug.

Between the years 1880 and 1920, a large number of windmills were constructed in Nebraska, Kansas and North and South Dakota which had wheels that measured from six feet to 60 feet in diameter. The wheels were elevated on towers as high as 100 feet to catch the wind. If the ranchers and farmers in these areas were to survive, they had to have fresh water. The windmills were the tools used to secure the water. Windmill weights were designed to serve as a counterbalance to the flywheel. Various windmill manufacturers needed a logo to distinguish their product from a competitor's and several decided to use cast iron chickens, squirrels, bulls and horses for easy identification. The three cast iron chickens all date from the late nineteenth century and were never painted..

The cast iron chicken is remarkably detailed. Many of the weights were hollow cast so the weight could be filled with sand or buckshot for ballast.

This squirrel was made by the Elgin Windmill Power and Pump Company of Elgin, Illinois. Squirrels are rarely found because the farmers, who had to chase them out of attics and corn cribs, had no desire to see them every day on their windmills.

This collection of windmill weights would require a great deal of time to duplicate. The "Fairbury" bull at right was made by the Fairbury Windmill Company of Nebraska. It weighs approximately 38 pounds and was used on ten and twelve foot windmills.

The hole in the body of the large chicken was used to pour in the ballast material.

The large Elgin "Mogul" rooster at above right carries a single coat of paint. Windmill weights with an original or early coat of paint are generally more valuable than weights without paint. In recent years, as the demand for weights has increased, there have been a number of reproductions cast. If a weight has paint that shows little or no wear, it is probably a positive step to keep your checkbook in your pocket. The Dempster #4 "short tailed" horse was made by the Dempster Manufacturing Company of Beatrice, Nebraska. This weight was used on a ten or twelve foot windmill. Short tailed horses are probably the most commonly found animal windmill weight. This example is unique because it carries a jointed jockey made of sheet metal that was aboard through many winters on the prairie.

This "Hanchett" bull was made by the Simpson Windmill and Machine Company in two halves that were bolted together. Weights were available from the company that were molded to the contours of the bull. The amount of weight was determined by the size of the windmill upon which it was placed.

The "Hummer" small chicken weighs approximately eight pounds and was made by the Elgin (Illinois) Windmill Power and Pump Company. The "Hummer Model L" was used on ten and twelve foot windmills and was obviously a big seller because many have survived and are still being added to collections. The four Hummers that follow all have slight variations in their surface that make each unique.

Detail of chicken windmill weight.

Chicken windmill weight.

Another chicken windmill weight with close-up view.

When we need a tooth pulled, transmission fixed, or drain unclogged, we go to a professional. We have all learned the hard way and tried to do it as cheaply as possible. In the long run, it's better to pay the price and move to something else. When that magic moment comes and it looks like a truly great weathervane will be joining the permanent collection, pause for a minute and then call a professional who can give something close to a definitive opinion about its value or age.

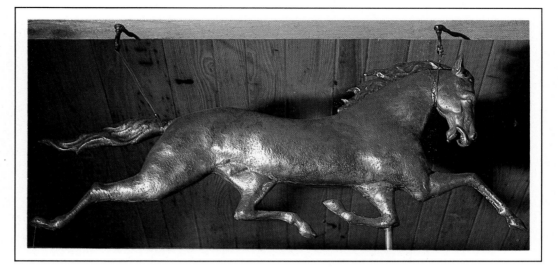

Trotting horse weathervane, copper, c. 1870-1900, 32″ long.

Milk cow weathervane, gilded copper, c. 1870-1900, 36″ long.

The quality of nineteenth century workmanship is best evidenced by a close look at the cow's underside. The reproductions tend to be more hastily executed and the oxidation that takes years to discolor a copper weathervane is sprayed on the reproductions. Over the years, there have been more reproduction weathervanes manufactured than there are roofs in New England on which to put them.

Copper cow weathervane that has oxidized over time, c. 1880-1900, 40″ long.

Rooster weathervane, oxidized copper, 28″ high, c. 1920.

Crowing rooster weathervane, extremely well made, 34″ high, c. early twentieth century.

Contemporary folk art weathervanes done by Pennsylvania artist Ivan Barnett are all signed. The major weathervane companies of Cushing, Washburne, and Fiske did not sign their products in the late nineteenth century and first quarter of the twentieth century. When weathervanes are faked, potassium sulphide is often used to blacken the copper and copper sulphate and acetic acid are applied to speed up the aging process and give it the greenish cast that old copper acquired over many years of exposure to the weather and air pollution.

These cast iron andirons of two baseball players probably date from the 1880's.

Early twentieth century swan chocolate mold.

Collection of late nineteenth century utility or all-purpose baskets made of oak and ash splint.

A survey of *Antique Magazine* advertisements from the 1920-1970 period will rarely turn up any mention of a basket for sale. They were not seriously collected until the early 1970's.

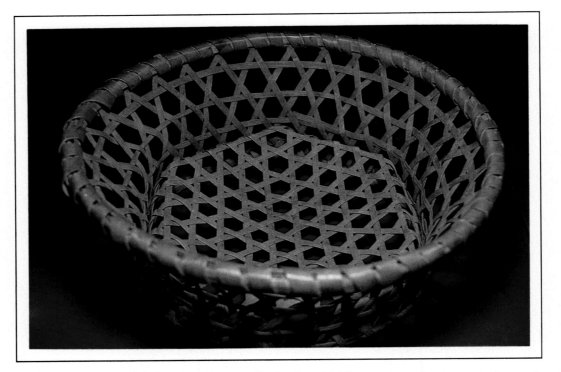

Shaker cheese or curd basket from New England. Cheese baskets were used to separate the curds from the whey.

Shaker storage basket made with oak splint.

Finely woven storage basket that was designed to be used on a table.

Tightly woven buttocks basket of oak splint that has been stained a chocolate brown. The handle is carved from a piece of hickory and bound or lashed to the rim of the basket.

Collection of country baskets. Painted baskets are considerably rarer and more valuable than the more commonly found unpainted examples.

Painted field basket of thickly cut splint. The heavy duty bow handles were designed to lift full loads.

Oak splint storage basket from New England that dates c. late nineteenth century.

Hiram Sibley seed box that was placed on a grocer's counter in the late nineteenth century. Seed "papers" or packets were priced for 5¢ and offered in wide variety.

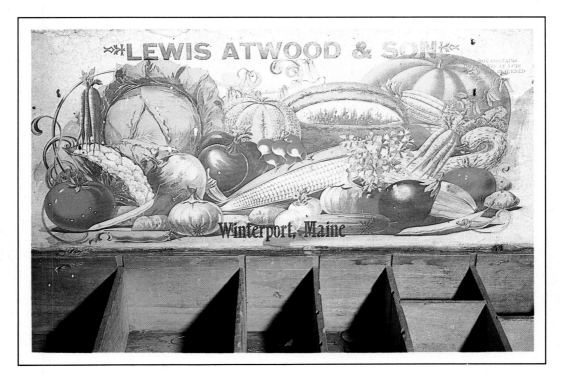

The critical factor in evaluating a seed box is usually the condition of the interior and exterior paper labels. This box from Winterport, Maine, is exceptional because of the elaborate interior label. Melons and vegetables in great color add much to the box.

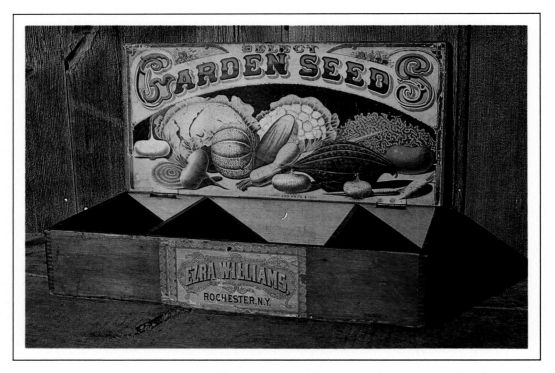

The Ezra Williams box from Rochester, New York, is another great example. The interior label is colorful and in excellent condition. Without the labels, the box would have minimal value.

A stack of seed boxes from New England is a difficult collection to accumulate. The most desirable boxes date from the 1860's to about 1900. After that point, the small seed companies were replaced by national concerns that mass-produced smaller oak boxes with more conventional labels.

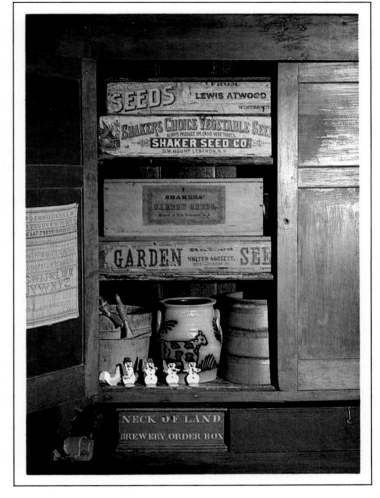

One-half of this blind front cupboard is filled with three Shaker seed boxes and a Lewis Atwood box.

Dated boxes and boxes that pre-date 1850 are rare. The Shakers and other smaller seed distributors delivered the boxes in the spring and came back to the store in the fall to retrieve them. Many boxes have a series of labels on top of one another.

The most sought after seed boxes were made by the Shakers. The New England Shakers were in the seed business until the early 1890's. At that point, they found they could not compete with firms that advertised and sold their seeds nationwide at discounted prices. The community at Mt. Lebanon, New York, was the largest producer of seeds of all the Shaker operations.

In addition to garden seeds, the Shakers had industries that offered doll bonnets, oval boxes, brushes and baskets. The strawberries were filled with ground pumice and used for sharpening needles. The surviving sisters at Canterbury, New Hampshire, still sell the strawberries.

The single object most identified with the Shakers is probably the oval box with "lappers" or fingers. The boxes were made of maple sides formed around a mold and a pine top and bottom. Wooden pins and copper rivets were used to hold the box together. It is a major financial effort to build a stack of boxes today. The primary factors in determining value are condition and color. If a box is painted blue, ochre (yellow) or bittersweet, it might necessitate mortgaging a child to buy an especially good one.

The Shakers offered the boxes in nests or stacks of five, seven, nine or twelve. Most were not painted before they were sold. Four of the boxes in this stack were not painted and the fifth was covered with a wash, which is a mixture of paint and water. The thinned paint allowed the grain of the wood to show through.

Shaker oval boxes constructed with a single finger or lapper are called "Harvard" boxes. They are alleged to have been made only in the Shaker community at Harvard, Massachusetts. The "Windsor" green paint was often used by the Shakers on oval boxes.

The five butter molds and the print are made of maple. They were made in a woodenware factory in the 1870-1890 period. The designs were impressed into the wood with a steel plate after the wood was steamed to make it pliable. The value of a mold or print is largely determined by the design it carries. Animals and birds are rare; pineapples and simple flowers are fairly common.

The Zero Creamery Buttermold was hand-carved rather than machine-impressed. The "bee hive" or "bell" was turned on a lathe. The cow is unusual because it has two leaves included in its design.

Machine-impressed cow buttermold with single leaf, fence and ground.

American eagles and other birds are considered rare. Both of these examples date from the late nineteenth century.

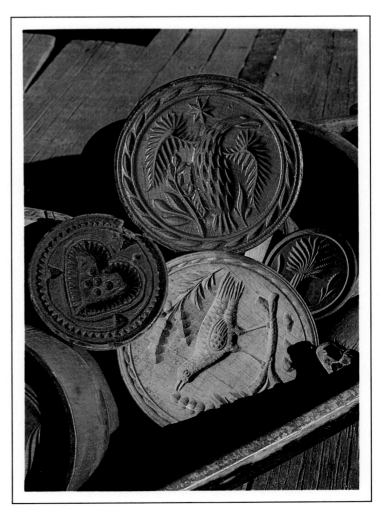

These Shaker pails were sold in the sisters' shop in most of their New England communities. The pails are made of pine staves held together with iron bands. The most distinctive characteristic of Shaker coopersware is the iron diamond used to brace the "drop" handle. These pails are normally painted and range in diameter from 3″ to 9″.

The storage barrel is made of pine staves that are bound by wooden bands. This example was never painted and dates from the early 1900's. The wheeled coffee grinder is the smallest size that the Enterprise Company produced. It is complete with its original drawer and eagle finial.

Sugar buckets or firkins were a standard feature in most late nineteenth and early twentieth century kitchens. They were made of pine staves and held together with wooden or metal bands. Grocers sold some filled with applesauce or mincemeat. In the home, they were used for storing sugar or flour. Like many factory-made household goods, they were available in huge quantities at low prices. When a lid was lost or a handle was broken, few were kept. Collectors try to build stacks of painted sugar buckets and face stiff competition for their pleasure. The serious problem begins when you want to top off the stack with smaller buckets.

Stacks can also be started with bail-handled pantry boxes and Shaker cheese boxes. Color is a critical factor in their price with blue being the highest in demand.

There are no standard sizes because hundreds of woodenware factories made firkins for consumers and businesses.

The firkin at left was sold filled with plums and still carries its original label. It dates from about 1900.

Painted dasher butter churns with pine staves and wooden bands date from about 1850-1875.

Shaker dasher butter churn with pine staves and "button hole" wooden bands. The bittersweet paint and the piggin handle make it an exceptional churn. A piggin handle is an extended stave that allowed the churn to be easily picked up with a single hand.

Twelve-drawer storage or spice chest made of pine that was hand-crafted rather than factory-made. Sears and Roebuck sold the mass-produced spice boxes well into the twentieth century with nailed construction, porcelain drawer pulls, and a single piece of wood for the back. This example dates from the third quarter of the nineteenth century.

This is another hand-crafted storage or spice chest that was made to rest on a counter rather than to be hung by a nail. The drawers are dovetailed; the piece dates from the mid-nineteenth century.

These wooden bowls are made of maple and were turned on a lathe. They were used as work bowls for chopping food or as mixing bowls. They were factory-made and date from the late nineteenth century. They have great color but most round wooden bowls eventually become oval due to shrinkage and crack across the grain.

Child's staved wash tub in blue paint and a miniature wooden wash board of pine.

There is an amazing variety of wash day equipment available to collectors. Wash boards can be found with tin, glass or wooden surfaces. This example is unusual because it is made of walnut. Typically the wooden boards were made of maple because it did not splinter, was durable and could survive lengthy contact with water.

Factory-made bread boards were sold by mail order houses as early as the 1870's. In recent years, there have been countless reproductions and European imports. The maple bowl with "Butter" machine-carved into it was a receptacle for a bowl of butter. "Bread" knives are more difficult to find than either bread boards or butter bowls.

Factory-made stocking stretchers should not be too difficult to find. Most were made of pine and have the size impressed into the wood.

Norwegian coffee mill of pine constructed to resemble a house. This initialed example could have been a wedding gift. It dates from about 1840-1860.

Lathe-turned pin cushion that screws onto a table top. The homespun cloth cover and the distinctive blue paint made this an exceptional piece.

Pine serving tray in blue paint, c. 1870.

Hand-crafted wooden chopping bowl in blue paint, found in Pennsylvania.

Maple chopping bowl in worn brown paint, found in Ohio, nineteenth century.

Any household article that is in constant use is extremely difficult to date with any degree of accuracy.

Pine carrier painted green, used to carry boxes of strawberries in from the field, late nineteenth-early twentieth century.

Pine carrier from a New England Shaker community, c. first half of the nineteenth century, never painted; held together with rosehead nails.

Norwegian bride's boxes were painted with colorful scenes and served as eagerly awaited gifts on nineteenth century wedding days.

If this antiques shop was in Nebraska or Peoria, it probably wouldn't play. It would be tough to sell lobster trap markers in both areas because the Platte and the Illinois Rivers are both lobstered out.

Phil Garlock, Central Illinois woodcarver, produces a variety of watermelons in his garden each summer and in his workroom each winter.

Pennsylvania woodcarver, Dan Strawser, produced the Santa Claus and the farm animals. We found the jointed man in a Connecticut antiques shop. He appears to date from the early twentieth century. It is extremely difficult to date wood carvings because the techniques used are the same today as they were a century ago. The next generation of collectors should face some interesting dilemmas.

Strawser's farm animals are remarkably close to scale, unlike many folk carvers whose work is often more whimsical in design.

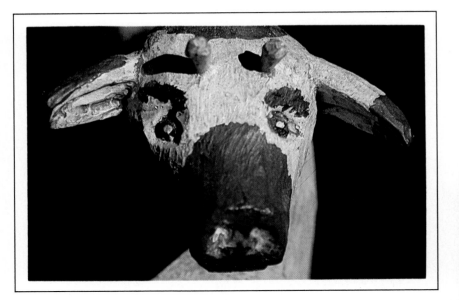

Wood-carved cow from Dan Strawser.

The painted birds are carved from pine, mounted on pointed sticks, and stuck into flower pots or country baskets.

Sheep carved by Larry Koosed.

Horse carved by an unknown folk artist.

These bears were limited editions from Steiff in 1980 and 1981.

The Steiff tea party was a limited edition in 1983.

The cow was created in 1977 by Charles and Jean Layland.

The rabbit, apples and baskets are the work of Pennsylvania artist, Ivan Barnett.

The scherenschnitte or paper cutting of the Brementown Musicians was done in 1981 by Massachusetts artist, Claudia Hopf.

Grouping of black dolls that date from the 1930's and 1940's.

The three dolls at left are newly made and the two at right date from the 1930-1950 period.

Black dolls, 1930's-1950's.

Wisconsin folk artist, Lou Schifferl, and his daughter, Pam, are two of the nation's premier wood carvers. The black lady was carved by Pam Schifferl.

The black man is a whirligig also done by Pam Schifferl.

Newspaper box from the *Chicago American* "Peach" edition, c. 1940's-1950's.

Copper barber shop sign with brass lettering, used in a hotel, c. late nineteenth century.

Grape Nuts cereal sign, used in a grocery store, c. early 1900's.

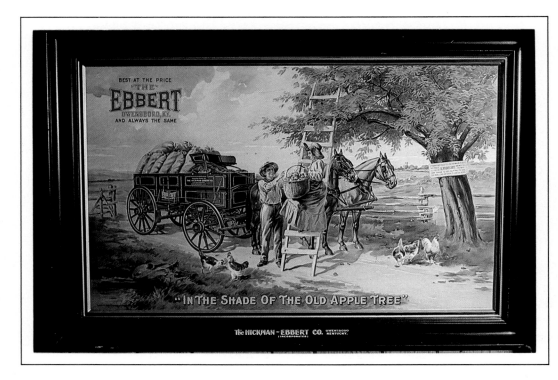

Metal "Ebbert" sign, advertising, c. early 1900's.

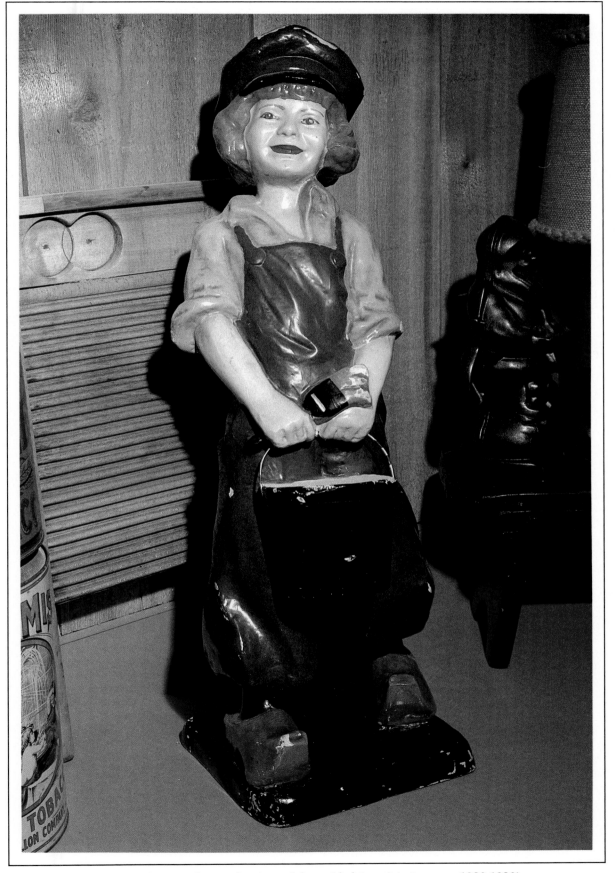

Little Dutch Boy, plaster-of-paris model provided to paint stores, c. 1920-1930's.

Lathe-turned barber pole, found in New York State, originally bracketed to the side of a building, c. early 1900's.

Hand-carved cigar store Indian, found in Washington State, c. 1900.

Pine restaurant sign, c. early 1900's.

Sheet metal sign originally nailed to exterior of grocery store in New York State, c. 1930's.

"Aroma" coffee bin, stenciled front, provided to stores by coffee company, c. 1920.

George Wallace Grocery sign, single 13-foot pine board with molding, Winchester, Illinois, c. 1935.

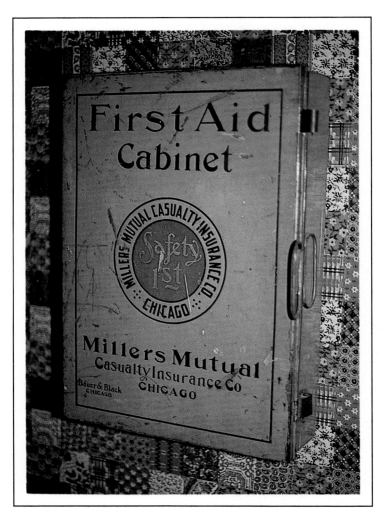

Metal first-aid cabinet provided to businesses by Millers Mutual Insurance Company, c. 1930.

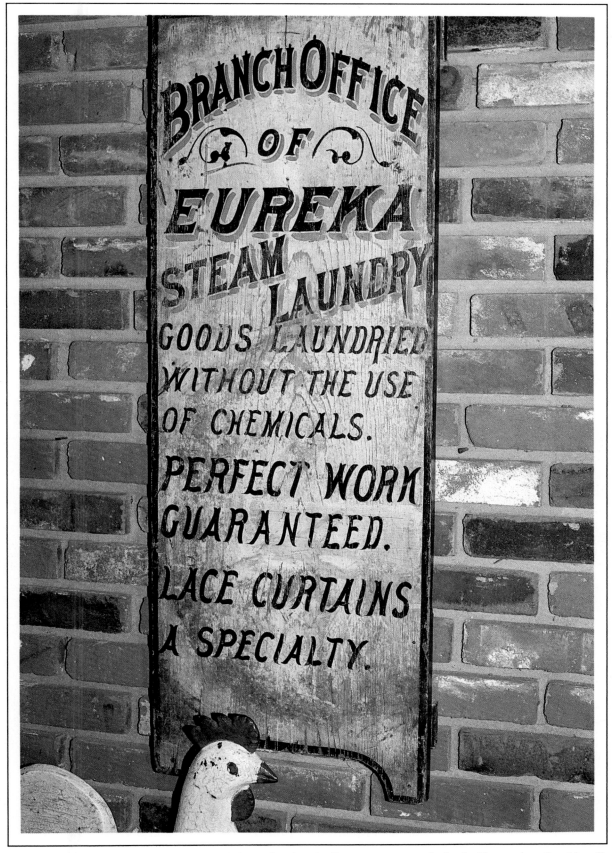

Eureka Steam Laundry sign, pine, originally hinged with a duplicate message on the back side, used on the sidewalk in front of the store, c. early twentieth century.

Mayo and Dixie Queen cut plug tobacco offered their product in six tins that were designed for collectors. The six "Roly Poly" tins include the Satisfied Customer, the Storekeeper, the Singing Waiter, Mammy, the Dutchman, and the Inspector or Man from Scotland Yard. The tins date from the 1912-1915 period.

This Man from Scotland Yard was one of the last in the series to be produced and is considered rare.

The Satisfied Customer is also part of the last series.

The Mammy tin was sold with Red Indian and U.S. Marine tobacco in addition to Mayo and Dixie Queen.

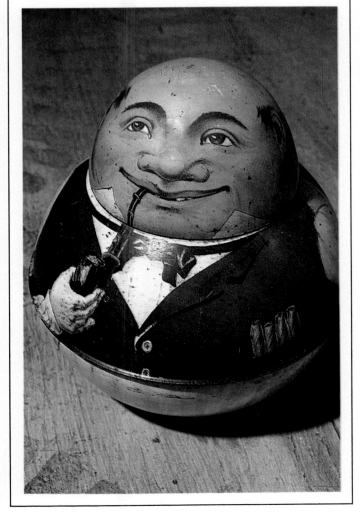

The Storekeeper.

The Shakers purchased bottles from the "world" and marketed their wide variety of food products throughout New England in the late nineteenth and early twentieth century.

The oversized Dr. Caldwell's box was used for display in a drug store in the early 1900's. The two other Caldwell boxes were offered to consumers who suffered from chronic irregularity.

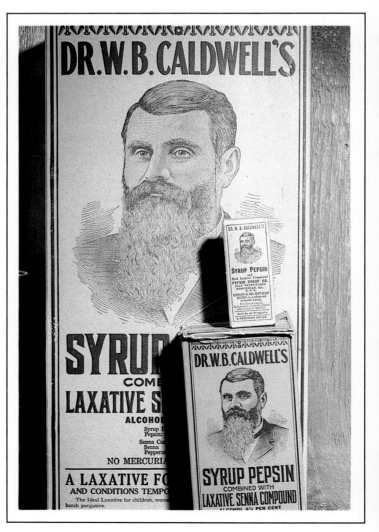

Labeled cow bells from the Collinsville, Illinois, foundry.

Carved pine eagle used as a wall hanging in an Ohio lodge hall, c. 1880.

Collection of American advertising tins and display items from the early 1900's.

There are a multitude of variations of Noah's Ark available to collectors. They were first made as toys in the early 1800's and continued to be offered by local craftsmen and manufacturers for more than a century. This ark and the numerous hand-carved and painted animals date from 1875-1900.

Doll given to Edna Goley Faulkner of Dupo, Illinois, as a first birthday gift in 1913.

Rocking horse of pine covered with horse hide and equipped with original saddle and tack, c. 1880-1910.

The horse and wheeled base can be removed from the rocker and pushed across the floor. The base and rocker are still in the original paint and stenciled decoration.

This rocking horse dates from the same time frame as the previous one shown but is not covered with hide. The pine is painted white and spotted black. The mane is horse hair.

This horse pull-toy is on a wheeled wooden base and stands 17″ high. It dates from the early 1900's.

Steiff is best known for Teddy bears but their wide variety of wheeled animals is equally collectable. This cow has the Steiff trademark button in its left ear.

Pig carved from pine and painted.

In the 1940's, the Ideal Toy Company made wind-up drummer boys in a variety of sizes. Few have survived to adulthood without having been overwound, thus losing their desire to perform.

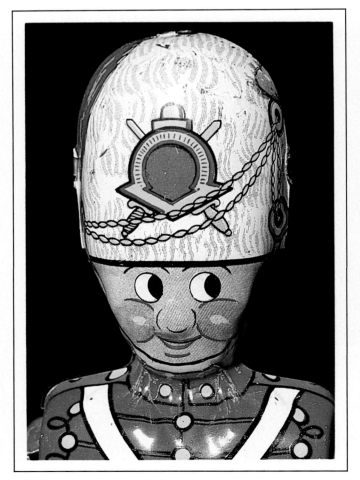

The Dog Patch Band wind-up toy is from the same period and in almost perfect condition.

The miniature circus cage wagon was made in Peru, Indiana, in 1884. It was originally in the extensive circus collection of Donald J. Raycraft.

Contemporary folk art dolls that appear to be considerably older than they are. Coffee and tea are occasionally used to darken the dolls and give the appearance of lengthy wear.

Simply constructed child's doll cradle that dates from the early 1900's. The blue paint adds significantly to its value.

Dressed rag doll and child's high chair made of pine and maple. The chair was made c. 1850-1870.

Late nineteenth century dressed doll from New England.

Child's pine sled from Maine stenciled and marked "Andrew", c. 1880-1910.

Mid-nineteenth century carved and dressed acrobatic clown that somersaults with a turn of the wrist.

Early twentieth century quilt from Pennsylvania.

The Ohio Amish quilt is dated "1917" and is the Carpenter Wheel pattern.

Quilts are in the same category as baskets because for many years they were not considered worthy of being collected. When the realization finally hit, the demand and prices for quilts went through the roof simultaneously. The comparison of baskets and quilts can also be made because both sometimes turn up in odd places at reasonable prices. Quilts and baskets were in use in homes all over the United States well into the twentieth century. There is no geographical limitation like there often is on pewter cupboards and duck decoys.

Wisconsin native, Vernona Sunvoldt, is nationally known for the lamps and shades she sells at antiques shows. The nineteenth century textiles she utilizes in the shades add much to their desirability.

It makes little sense to use old homespun for curtains when quality reproduction fabric at reasonable prices is available. We feel the same way about chairs and couches. With escalating prices, the day of the purist who refuses to mix old and new is about over. Only a very limited number of collectors will spend several thousand dollars for a chair frame and then a similar amount to have it covered with period fabric.

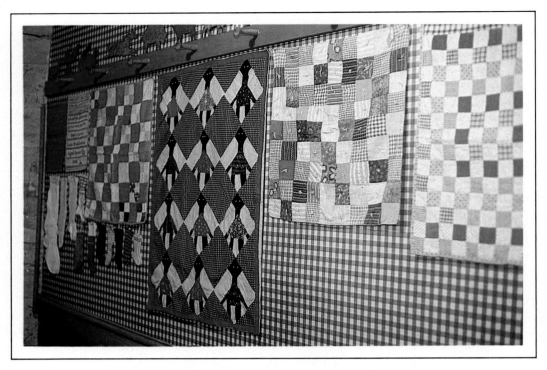

Collection of twentieth century crib quilts.

The children's woolen socks are from the 1880-1910 period and make an interesting collection.

The tin quilt patterns were made by Ivan Barnett.

This bunting was sold in variety stores in the early twentieth century for holiday and patriotic celebrations. We were in Houston for an elaborate antiques show and were amazed at the prices on much of the country furniture and accessories on display. The bunting was in the corner of a booth and the dealer replied "Eight" when asked the price. We were conditioned to eight hundred and eight thousand from our travels around the show and the "eight" ($8) seemed incongruous.

The hooked rug dates from the 1930's.

Collection of nineteenth century linen and cotton homespun.

Nineteenth century linen bed tick that was filled with feathers and slept on or under.

Contemporary folk art canvas floor cloth made by Carol Raycraft.

One of the best things about Christmas at our house is the annual unwrapping of the Schifferel Santa Claus carvings. Several of us have voted in the past to break out the carvings in July but we always get out voted by the traditionalists who hold out until September.

This Santa Claus was done by Pam Schifferel who is equally as skillful with paint brush as knife. Many contemporary woodcarvers have one of the skills but few have both.

The English Santa Claus was carved by Lou Schifferel.

The detail of the toys in the English Santa's bag is exceptional.

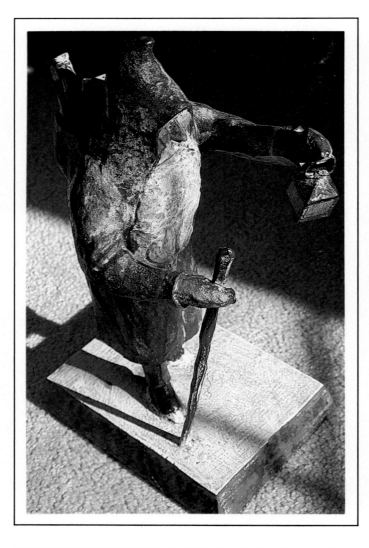

Another contemporary Santa.

Wood carvings, left to right, of Koosed, Strawser and the two Schifferels.

The 7-foot artificial Christmas tree is a "feather" tree that dates from the 1900-1915 period. The green pine needles on the tree are actually chicken feathers that have been dyed and glued to the branches. The trees were made in heights ranging from 12″ to 7′. The majority were imported from Germany and designed to be set on a table top.

Several years ago, there was little demand for antique Christmas ornaments. A series of articles in the country-oriented magazines created an instant demand and prices quickly spiraled. It is still possible to find old ornaments inexpensively priced at flea markets and estate or house sales when attics are emptied.

This contemporary Santa Claus appears to be passed out on the morning of December 26.

The Koosed Santa Claus and the smaller Strawser example are both well done. The horse is the work of Ivan Barnett.

The paper Christmas ornaments are done by Claudia Hopf.

Price Guide

No values are listed for contemporary country items.

Page 7
  Pine Cupboard $2,200.00-2,500.00
Page 8
  Pine step-back cupboard $1,500.00-1,800.00
Page 9
  Norweigian cupboard $1,200.00-1,500.00
  Painted pine cupboards . . . . each $1,500.00-2,000.00
Page 10
  Chimney Cupboard $700.00-850.00
Page 11
  Step-back cupboard $1,300.00-1,500.00
Page 12
  Pine open cupboard $1,100.00-1,300.00
Page 13
  Child's dish dresser $600.00-750.00
Page 14
  Poplar jelly cupboard $575.00-675.00
  Pine open cupboard $1,200.00-1,300.00
Page 15
  Step-back cupboard $2,000.00-2,800.00
Page 16
  North Carolina open cupboard $1,400.00-1,600.00
Page 17
  Pine open cupboard $1,200.00-1,400.00
Page 18
  New England chimney cupboard $475.00-575.00
Page 19
  Pine farm table $1,600.00-1,800.00
  Hanging cupboard $500.00-575.00
Page 20
  Pie safe $500.00-600.00
Page 21
  Pine pie safe $900.00-1,100.00
Page 22
  Hired man's bed $1,200.00-1,400.00
Page 23
  Low post bed $1,100.00-1,500.00
  High post bed $1,500.00-1,800.00
Page 24
  Sugar chest $750.00-825.00
  Blanket box $1,500.00-1,800.00
Page 25
  Blanket box $800.00-1,100.00
  Blanket box $900.00-1,200.00
Page 26
  Grain-painted blanket box $1,000.00-1,200.00
Page 27
  Pine dry sink $1,200.00-1,400.00
  Pine dry sink $800.00-1,000.00
Page 28
  Pine dry sink $1,450.00-1,600.00
Page 29
  Pine bucket bench $400.00-500.00
Page 30
  Pine bucket bench $300.00-375.00
  Walnut desk $850.00-1,150.00
Page 31
  Plantation desk $1,800.00-2,200.00
Page 32
  Lift-top desk $675.00-950.00
Page 33
  School master's desk $1,000.00-1,300.00
  Rocking chair $150.00-185.00
Page 34
  Spindle-back chair $225.00-275.00
  Rocking chair $350.00-450.00
Page 35
  Country sofa $675.00-900.00
  Kitchen chair $200.00-225.00
Page 36
  Mammy's bench $1,200.00-1,400.00
  Shaker No. 7 rocking chair $1,200.00-1,400.00

Page 37
  Child's arm chair $700.00-850.00
  Side chair $225.00-275.00
Page 38
  Ladder-back chair $200.00-250.00
  Step-back cupboard $1,400.00-1,600.00
Page 39
  Saw-buck work table $800.00-1,000.00
  Side or lamp table $400.00-550.00
Page 40
  Farm table $850.00-1,150.00
  Carpenter's table $750.00-900.00
Page 41
  Hunt table $500.00-650.00
  Stretcher based table $775.00-975.00
Page 42
  Cobbler's bench $450.00-550.00
  Painted boxes . . . . each $385.00-500.00
Page 43
  Spool cabinet $600.00-800.00
Page 44
  Dry sink $1,000.00-1,200.00
Page 45
  Stoneware butter churn $600.00-675.00
Page 46
  Stoneware jar $800.00-900.00
Page 47
  Slip-trailed crock $1,400.00-1,700.00
Page 48
  Decorated crock $2,000.00-3,000.00
Page 49
  Stoneware jar $375.00-400.00
  Decorated crock $525.00-600.00
Page 50
  Four gallon crock $800.00-1,000.00
Page 52
  Decorated crocks . . . . each $325.00-375.00
Page 54
  Stenciled storage jar $425.00-600.00
Page 55
  Stoneware butter churn $200.00-275.00
  Slip-decorated pie plate $275.00-350.00
  Redware milk pan and pitcher $600.00-800.00
Page 56
  Sponge-decorated stoneware $125.00-325.00
Page 57
  Rockingham stoneware $175.00-350.00
  Stoneware pigs . . . . each $150.00-250.00
Page 58
  Rockingham stoneware pitchers . . . . each $450.00-650.00
Page 60
  Graniteware pitcher and bowl set $200.00-300.00
Page 61
  Stoneware jug $250.00-300.00
Page 62
  Chicken windmill weights $1,000.00-1,200.00, $600.00-800.00,
                                              $400.00-600.00 (smallest)
Page 63
  Squirrel windmill weight $1,200.00-1,400.00
Page 65
  Horse w/jockey windmill weight $1,200.00-1,400.00
Page 66
  Bull windmill weight $1,200.00-1,400.00
Page 67
  Chicken windmill weight $400.00-475.00
Page 68
  Chicken windmill weight $500.00-575.00
Page 69
  Chicken windmill weight $425.00-475.00
Page 70
  Chicken windmill weight $500.00-575.00
Page 71
  Horse weathervane $1,300.00-1,600.00
  Milk cow weathervane $2,000.00-3,000.00